Tennessee Landscape
with
Blighted Pine

Poems

Jesse Graves

Tennessee Landscape
with
Blighted Pine

Poems

Jesse Graves

Texas Review Press
Huntsville, Texas

FIRST EDITION

Requests for permission to acknowledge material from this work should be sent to:

Permissions
Texas Review Press
English Department
Sam Houston State University
Huntsville, TX 77341-2146

Acknowledgements:

The author gratefully acknowledges the publications where poems in this collection first appeared, sometimes in slightly different form:

Aethlon, Appalachian Heritage, Bat City Review, Connecticut Review, descant, Kestrel, Louisiana Literature, Motif: Writing by Ear, New Millennium Writings, Now & Then, Pembroke Magazine, Pisgah Review, Potomac Review, Prairie Schooner, Shawangunk Review, Shepherd Anthology of Appalachian Literature, South Carolina Review, The Southern Poetry Anthology, Volume IV: Louisiana, Southern Poetry Review, Southern Quarterly, Sow's Ear Poetry Review, Still: The Journal, Tar River Poetry, Texas Review, Town Creek Poetry, Tusculum Review

Special thanks are due Arthur Smith and William Wright, who read all of the poems in this book more than once, and to Marilyn Kallet, Jeff Daniel Marion, and Robert Morgan, who have mentored my work from the beginning. Many more friends have made invaluable suggestions for the revision and arrangement of these poems, and I owe them a debt of gratitude; they include Amy Billone, Joseph Campana, Thomas Alan Holmes, Judy Loest, Linda Parsons Marion, Deb Scaperoth, Steve Sparks, and Randall Wilhelm. I had the incredible good fortune to study with A.R. Ammons and Jack Gilbert at key moments in my life, and I will be forever grateful for their wisdom and encouragement. Finally, these poems are infused with memories of my grandmothers, Edith Houston and Bonnie Rouse, my uncle Gerald Graves, my brother Nick Bruner, and Loie, the golden retriever at my side while virtually all of these poems were written. They are lost to me in body, but not in love and spirit.

Cover Design: Chad M. Pelton
Frontispiece: Peg Hambright
Author Photo: Lisa Graves

Library of Congress Cataloging-in-Publication Data
Graves, Jesse, 1973-
Tennessee landscape with blighted pine : poems / Jesse Graves. ~ 1st ed.
    p. cm.
ISBN 978-1-933896-71-7 (pbk. : alk. paper)
I. Title.
PS3607.R38625T46 2011
811'.6~dc23
                                2011033951

This book is for my cornerstones:

Hugh and Joyce Graves
Lisa and Chloe Graves

Contents

9   For the Frozen Wood

I

11   Tennessee Landscape with Blighted Pine
14   River Gods
15   Firing Order
17   At Seven
18   Digging the Pond
19   Elegy for a Hay Rake
20   Johnson's Ground
22   St. Paul

II

27   The Night Café: North Rendon, New Orleans
29   Detroit Muscle
30   His Confession
31   Sparrow
32   The Donkey on the Road
33   Emissaries
34   Bayou Storm
36   Elemental Study
37   Wrightsville Beach
38   Time and the Motions Our Bodies Made
39   The Road into the Lake
41   Morning Sky, September 2001
42   Understory

III

45   For Richard Wilbur

47   The Pier at 5 AM

48   Wild Strawberries at St. Mary's Hospital

50   Piano Key

51   Reservation Snapshot

52   Devil's Snuff

53   Facing West from Cumberland Gap

54   Trade

55   Revivals

56   Little Girl and the Dreadful Snake

57   Water Washing Away

58   Mother's Milk

60   The Upper Ridge

IV

63   Field Portrait

65   Late Summer Woodcut

66   My Sister at Sea

67   Temper in a Time of War

68   Vista

69   Search Program

70   Equations

71   The Wilderness Trail

72   Nightjar Songs

73   Wellsprings

74   Echolalia

76   Deep Corner

77   Big Elm Point

For the Frozen Wood

At dawn, drifting snow gave the sky back
to itself brighter than its first falling,
inviting some fool out to stand slack,
watch the slow light come crawling

to itself brighter than the first falling.
I'm the perfect fool for a day like this
watching the slow light come crawling,
erasing the ground's darkened canvas.

Some would call me a fool for saying this,
but I hear their voices and see lost faces
rising from the ground's dark canvas,
my dear ones searching for their places.

I hear soft voices and see loss in faces
shaped like hollow versions of my own,
my departed searching for the places
where their bodies faltered and went down

in shapes like hollow versions of my own,
inviting some fool out to stand slack
where their bodies faltered and went down
at dawn, snow giving what the sky takes back.

I

Tennessee Landscape with Blighted Pine

Dry summer and the upper field quiet at noon.
Spring's green pirouette tangled in barbed wire,
Its promise snapped like matchsticks, burnt-orange
Pine needles cracking loose from stiff joints,
                                        Silence dropped so low
It rings like a bell's soft echo.

Here once was a boy running with a black and white half-shepherd dog,
Hair summer-blonde, hands darkened to rust by wet clay
                                        Rummaged for arrowheads.

No fear then but the darting tongues of timber snakes:

That certainty lost to whatever passes for time,
                        The ground skipped beneath his feet.

   *   *   *

Once I stood here through a mid-day snowfall, sky staring and nearly dark,
Watching my shoes sink in the white sheets,
Petals of frozen clouds feathering down through my eyelashes.
            Home from college, free of abnormal psychology
And media arts, endless boredoms that passed for a life of the mind.

Not a sound that whole afternoon, nothing more alive than my breath,
            Silence in the snowy field, the heavy trees,
Known in sense but not by name, nothing really known by name.

   *   *   *

No one came here to build the perfect city.
They came out of Philadelphia and before that New York,
            Before that Baden-Baden and the Palatinate.

A narrow river unspooled out of the mountains, Alamance County,
                            Western Carolina, and washed them up
Before what must have seemed God's own promise:
            Tall fescue and cleft hoofprints of deer on the muddy banks.

Here they could harvest what grew, tear life out of the ground.

They started with trees, built a lumber-mill and floated log-rafts downriver
To settlements in Rockwood, Oliver Springs, and Chattanooga—

1792.

Already the name had been lightened to Graves, and only old Johannes,
Born 1703 in the Rhineland, still kept himself Graff.

            *   *   *

Left alone, indoors, I tend toward sounds not found
In the open field, *Sotto voce* of Mahler's *Misterioso Symphony*,
            Surge and retreat of John Coltrane's *Crescent*.

No analogue in nature, no precedent in the high branches.

One night in Faubourg Marigny I heard Kidd Jordan ignite the air
With a tenor saxophone.
            It sounded like ashes falling, each speck a thousand pounds.

            *   *   *

Life abounds on the perimeter, overflushes the fencerows
            Most years, honeysuckle lacing the cedar posts,
But now the heat beats its odd rhythms and the billion tiny teeth
            Of the blight work through this zone and the next,
Leaving orange skeletons standing over variegated shadows.

Chestnuts once shouldered this ridgeline, owned the horizons
From Sharps Chapel to Jellico Mountain, on past the blue smudge
                            Of Clinch Mountain to the east.

Impossible to picture it today, three generations after aphids
    Cut through them—
        Floorboards and ceiling joists, finely-grained paneling
In the old houses the only proof that an existence
    Once so sturdy could vanish
                Like clouds into clouds.

                *   *   *

So many years ago a man toiled here, clearing and reaping the barest life.
    How many years?
        The years themselves do not know, do not count turns
            In their circle.

Before Lincoln, before Darwin, before Marx.
        One of his sons killed in the field by an Indian.

An X by "His Mark" on the deed. An X by "His Wife's Mark."

The words Jesse Graves quilled below it in the practiced hand of a magistrate.

                *   *   *

The dead move through us at their will, their voices chime
    Just beyond our hearing.
How else do we feel our names when no one speaks them?
How else catch the echo of footprints two decades
    After running through the grass?

Alone in the field, and never alone. Quiet and not quiet.
                Home and away.

River Gods

In the lapse-time of remembering, my life
folds back through the warp of this city
the way the Tennessee River winds through it,

and I live again on the north bank, in Maplehurst,
watching the slow seep of barges downriver,
my blood renewed and coursing old arteries again.

Years break apart, become sediment in the stream
of those distant days, their blue-lobed nights.
Twenty-two and alive only to feel.

Still, I dared it only once, walking the rail trestle
where Cormac McCarthy's hillbilly Ulysses
docked the houseboat and dragged his trawling line.

Since no one wants to cheat a foolish death alone,
I convinced my friend to leave his satchel on the bank
and we stepped out a hundred feet over the night.

We sprang from tie to tie, hoping for solid wood,
for no rumbling train engine beyond the south hill,
our nerve soldered by a half-pint of Maker's Mark.

Lights from downtown Knoxville laced bright letters
across the water, and we stood, staring down
into a floating book, our bodies swaying like kites,

far above the circulations of ancient, whiskered fish,
held aloft by the confluence of blind river gods.
So much of the unknown rushing beneath us.

Firing Order

I

We found no warmth under the open hood,
Stranded mid-field where the truck's engine failed.
This work preceded all other, hay baled,
Stacked high and waiting on the metal bed.
Cows in winter, like broken furniture leaned
Against a wall, braced in zippery wind,
Staring out from their mysterious minds,
Hipbones like arched frames carved from wood.

My job was simple: I held the wrench
While his fingers set to work pulling wires,
Clearing rust and debris from the engine
Block, pocket knife flashing quick and sure.
His hands in the open heart of a machine,
Old plugs scraped clean enough to carry fire.

II

The field reveals no human history,
Logs none of the hours my father spent
Disking its soil, sowing down seeds, back bent
Like a tire iron, his fair neck blistered.
Bitt Rouse's sleeve once caught in the corn thresh
Keeps us careful, mindful of accidents—
Blood spilled here seeps through webs of buried roots.
Subsoil remembers, but topsoil forgets:

Forty summers ago, high heat of June
Salting the air, a young man's good right hand,
The one that bowed his famous fiddle tunes,
Churned to paste well before the pain began,
His feet tearing marks like ancient runes
Etched in the dirt, his signature on that land.

III

Under the pond's frozen face bright florets
Of algae swirl out and spread through the wild
Energy of their iced-over lives,
Deeper cold approaching with sunset.
Late November drawing down, so much less
Than it started with, early cold, crops shriveled,
The leaves tell it all in luminous wreckage.
He remembers, and I do, but the ground forgets.

What work gets done today will come again
Tomorrow, the day after, on and on,
Until he gives out, and the ground reclaims
What my father and I set in motion,
An engine turning, our family name
Stamped on the place that takes us back in.

At Seven

Every morning, morning's measure: breakfast early, then play,
Flashing across the porch with cats or soldiers' planes,
Their metal wings armed with tiny machine guns
And stamped with a Union Jack or the Stars and Bars.

The side yard stretched into the beaches at Normandy
Or else Fenway Park, baseball cards taking the field,
Pennant races played out with nickels and a wooden pencil.

The pre-structure of summer days, as before the terrible
Arrival of chalkboards, homework, and long stillness,
Table and chair and child all bolted together.

What work there was involved the grass and a loud
Engine, its fumes turning circles in the nose and behind
The eyes, or an open pocketknife through strands of twine,
Straw-bales loosened and scattered over the seedling beds.

Digging the Pond

The vision must have come after rain,
a picture of water standing so deep
a house could hide under it.
He pushed and dug and cut through
scrub pines like they were tall blades of grass,
dragged orange clay from under the topsoil.

At thirteen, I mostly stood back and waited
for rocks to lug into the nearest gulley,
sinking my hands under the cool mud
so long buried, the runoff from two ridges—
we found an arrowhead the first day
and envisioned bone shards and lead slugs.

For years a hard rain would spill its banks,
and pond lilies would sheen it with yellow
through the warm months, before the drought
years and turtles did their work, and its water
looked like something caught in a rusted bucket.

When my father stands on the bank and talks
over what to do with the farm, he looks up
toward the ridge-line and down at cracked dirt.
He can name every species of tree, wild root,
the compounds of the soil in every field,
and knows that I stood off to the side too often
to learn what he was born knowing.
The doing and the undoing.
I can find in his face what he reads
about the future in the tea-colored water,
his eyes and mine trying to avoid it.

Elegy for a Hay Rake

To every thing its season, and to every tool
its final turn; to the Farmhand rake my father
bought hard-used in 1976, rust has eaten away
all your labels, all your sheen and simple function;
to what I hope is my last sight of you, unhitched
and standing in the field like a photograph
from the Great Depression;
                                        farewell to the cut hay left
scattered on the ground to rot, nothing ate you
but the soil that birthed you; to the tractor tire
those long grappling points missed by inches
on every sharp turn, you survived without puncture;
to the long afternoon hours spent digging clumps
out of the balers' clenched teeth, good money
cannot buy you back;
                                        so long to the lucky machine,
lucky I won't sell you as an antique, that no one will
paint you red, white, and blue and plant you in a garden,
or hang you on a restaurant wall; goodbye to the five
leaning wheels, their crooked tines turning, reaching up
like broken fingers to wave hello, hello, goodbye.

Johnson's Ground

We sit under the awning and watch them descend in unison.
A flock of thirty or more down through the heavy rain
We weren't supposed to get, pecking where grass is thin
For what the moisture turns up.
                              They look like the sound of the word
Grackle, these scavengers with wings muted black as painted iron rails,
As wet tar, their empty beaks flashing a bright citrus smear.
Memorial Day weekend and the weather drives us for cover,
Beating down plastic flowers and darkening the family gravestones.

Each year we arrive, like any family, to admire new babies
And find out who has changed jobs or gotten married,
I come to see who's left to sit in the shaded chairs
Where my grandmother sat with her oldest sister Minnie
For the last time, neither of them able to name the other,
But both staring as if into a clouded mirror.
                              In the memory of their faces
I see pillars of stone, pillars of stippled salt,
Where the hammer of time drives the chisel of living,
The opaque blue of their eyes, each pair reflecting the other,
Sky blue buttons threaded through a dark blue dress.

Homecoming at the cemetery: they never let us go, even the ones
Laid under before our births continue to make their claims,
To draw the interest on their spent lives.
                              My grandfather waits here,
A Houston buried in Johnson ground—such is the appointment
He made with them. He was dead two years before
I was born, but who do I remind the old people of?
Whose picture did I stare into above the living room fireplace?

My great-uncle Gene tells my father and me about the base
He served in Korea, how bombs sounded hitting the village,
While a hundred feet away is my cousin Gary,
killed in Vietnam, telling his story into our other ears,
into the soles of our shoes.
                              The foraging birds drag worms

Out of the ground; we pull dark meat from the bones
Of chicken thighs and split boiled potatoes with plastic forks.

Damp air hums in our lungs and old people begin
Covering dishes—the rain always seeps in,
Even under shelter.
                              I offer my hands one more time
To the company who packs their leftovers and drives away,
And to the company who stays behind, under the tall grass,
Left in the restless turning of what we remember of them.

St. Paul

"How cold you think it is out there?" Gerald asked,
and I said that I couldn't tell, pretty cold, I guessed.
The fog my breath made on the side window
told me all I wanted to know about the temperature.
We drove north on Highway 61 past Hannibal, Missouri
when the rain we had trailed since western Kentucky
started to clink on the windshield.
The sky darkened gradually, and soon
the range of the headlights was as far as I could see.
The raindrops suddenly thickened in the light,
and my throat felt a little tighter.

Our Kris Kristofferson tape jammed the third time
through "Sunday Morning Coming Down"
and wouldn't play or eject from the 8-track player,
so Gerald started telling me about his run-in
with an army lieutenant when he was stationed
in Okinawa and danced with the wrong Mama-san.
But as the snow became undeniable,
the story trailed off before any real action,
and then for a while the only sound was the suck
of breath through his unfiltered Camels.
I had heard about the lieutenant before, how he
grabbed Gerald's nose and twisted him to the ground,
that his face had never felt the same after that.

*   *   *

We had three hundred crates of navel oranges and tangerines
in the trailer and had stopped for nothing but diesel fuel
since we left Clearwater, Florida yesterday at noon.
We were due in St. Paul, Minnesota at ten o'clock in the morning.

*   *   *

Gerald had been on the road for eleven days,
stopping at home once to wash his clothes
and pick me up for the rest of this run.
He had called from Michigan, like he always did
after a few days up north.
He said our voices sounded like driving back home.
Gerald was my favorite uncle, and he talked to me
like I might actually know something,
                    which none of the other grown-ups did.

                    *   *   *

We parked in a long row of trucks a hundred yards
from the front of the Flying J Truckstop on Exit 219,
and the whisper of all the idling engines
contrasted with the excitement of the drivers' voices
as they talked about the blizzard moving down from Iowa.
The muscles down the backs of my legs trembled
as I stepped out of the truck, and as Gerald disappeared
among a crowd lingering beside the fuel pumps,
the snow fanned red in the gleam of pulsing brake lights.

                    *   *   *

We fueled the rig and filled Styrofoam cups with coffee,
then headed back across the parking lot through the snow.
Fewer trucks were rolling in, and even the freshest tire tracks
were almost covered as we pulled back onto the highway.
We laughed and joked all through dinner, mostly
about near-misses Gerald had driven through, but now
on the road we were quiet until we saw police lights up ahead,
and a state trooper standing in front of a barricade
made us get out of the cab, to prove to us that the snow
was already past the ankles of our boots.

When we were back in the truck, Gerald folded open
an atlas to find some county route that would take us
around the road block. My uncle was what cops and teachers
and branch managers hated, and exactly what I was trying
to become. He looked like Robert Redford playing
Jeremiah Johnson, someone who didn't care that he needed
a shave and haircut, who seemed free to get up and leave.

We ended up sleeping in the truck on the exit ramp,
piling extra shirts for blankets, and I was secretly glad
to be shut down until daylight. In the evenings,
when I was a child, we would wait until my mother
went to bed, then sneak out into the side yard and sit
on the hood of Gerald's car looking up at the stars.
The white boards of the house hovered under a blue glow,
but the interior was dark as the night woods, and if there were
no clouds, the constellations blinked us their messages.

*   *   *

I learned in Tennessee History class that two hundred million
years ago our whole valley lay at the bottom of a great ocean,
that all of the world I had seen sat underwater for an eternity.

*   *   *

A green valley under a murky sea. The rumor of an Indian
burial ground hidden in the hollers in Capps' Creek.
Sandy blonde hair of Angie Holloway.

The Ernie & Bernie Show playing for the UT basketball team
on AM radio. "Crystal" printed on a name tag
at a truckstop in southeast Missouri.

So many dreams kept me occupied that spring and summer
until I went to work at Standard Knitting Mill in the fall.
After we delivered the fruit at the warehouse in Minnesota,

we ran empty to Chicago and picked up a load
heading south. I drove some of the long flat stretches
through Indiana, but other than my father's International flatbed

in haying season, I never drove another truck after that trip.
Before long, Gerald was hauling with a tank line,
no passengers allowed, and he was home every weekend,

talking still about how he hated driving trucks,
wishing he had kept to carpentry and woodwork.
There was a shed behind the little house he bought that he talked

about turning into a workshop, but now so many years
after he has died, nearly a decade, the door to that shed
just hangs by the hinges, nothing inside but old tires,

grease-rags from uniform shirts and dish towels, and a solid block
of light from a high window, the cracked one that must
have let the unfinished future, half a life of chairs, shelves,
and bedframes never built, seep out and away.

II

The Night Café: North Rendon, New Orleans

If we felt generous with ourselves, we drank well,
Basil Hayden's at eight dollars a glass if Les ordered,

Marker's Mark at five-fifty if the tab was mine.
Most of the tables leaned vacantly against their chairs,

The walls exhaling a low shade of green, the kind of room
Van Gogh said a man could lose his mind in.

Our talking threaded through the light and into the dark.
We argued the catalogues of the not-quite-Bob-Dylans—

Then always into further obscurities and personal abstractions,
Tenderness for the women we loved before our wives,

How those romances added up to lives someone chose against;
Entire books we conceived in dreams but did not write, a travelogue

Of the Yucatan Peninsula, a study of empire in Herodotus;
The children we could have had playing in watery shadows

Beneath the billiard tables, watching for a sign of recognition,
Waiting for the names we never gave them to be called.

Whatever failures we recounted would never be trapped
Inside the sweat-rings our cold glasses left on the tabletop,

Their consequences wiped away with the back of a hand.
In the maroon glint of the bathroom's single hanging bulb,

The breasts of vintage centerfolds shone like the night sky
Above Athens just after the Persians torched the city.

We felt our nearest experiences with death and transcendence
Equal to the siege at Thermopylae, captured in our own *Histories*,

Recorded beneath swirls of smoke at a bar on North Rendon,
In the hope of thereby preserving from decay the remembrance

Of what men have done—thus the story opens, told like every tale
That regrets where its ends, murky light rising above the forsaken city.

Detroit Muscle

I cranked the Camaro by sparking two ignition wires
and the engine rumbled like a death foretold.
Billy Thatcher rebuilt it with Knoxville Motor Speedway
in mind, and got as far as an Edelbrock Torquer intake,
Holley four-barrels, and a pistol-grip gear shifter
before his money ran out and he sold it to my dad.

For a full year I had passed it twice a day on the school bus,
marking its progress from a primered shell on cinderblocks
beside Thatcher's garage, to something like a balled fist
on wheels, a '69 Rally Sport, the very spirit of Detroit labor.
I had glued together its exact replica on my bedroom floor.

We spent a summer tuning up the 350 until it hummed,
and my uncle painted it the blue of a thunderstorm at dusk.
The car sounded like lightning striking when I pulled
onto the highway—it could lay streaks on the blacktop
all through first gear and catch it again hitting second.

I opened it up one day on a gravel road in Sharps Chapel,
windows down, "Statesboro Blues" blasting from the stereo,
and I lost it—the front tire slipped the road and I went
spinning, one ditch swallowed me up and spit me straight
into the other and I landed upside down in a tobacco field,
wondering where the road went and why I wasn't on it.

His Confession

I expected the worst when Paul tucked the pistol in his belt.
Midsummer night, light wind:
                    it all suggested the road, open air.

A '76 Ducati doesn't thunder so much as express pure
                    high-pitched menace, falcon to a fieldmouse.

His confession: he still loves the girl at the record store.

Anybody can go to Mead's Quarry now.
A nature center bought the land,
                              made it public,
but when we rode out we had to pry
a fence open and roll the motorcycle through.

Midnight. One AM. Light-headed, heavy-limbed
                    on the cheapest beer at Kenjo Market.

He said, *I keep writing songs about her,*
                    I call the store every night she works.

Forget it, I said, *it's a bad idea. It's poison.*

She's laid half the guys who work there, he said.
                    What about you?

We took turns blasting bright eruptions
                              out of the water,
echoes hitting the pink marble face,
          bouncing back at us like live fire.

The sounds sobered us—
                    we thought of houses close by.

Fun's over, he said, dragging the bike out of the weeds,
          but that God-damned moon's so full
                              we should have shot it.

Sparrow

Flickering around the compost heap,
swirled dust bunny, swept up & pitched out
clanging a song I could forget in 10 seconds.
You land in anything and somehow find
a morsel, undigested seed in a jay's droppings,
blind pink face of an earthworm underneath.

Hardly worth an ode, hardly
demanding a full line of thought.
Persistent, though, not quiet in the cage
evolution built for you—
your *blip-blip-buzzzz* a steady comment.
What about? Well, nothing really,
announcing sex, food, some early warning,
nothing in it said for me.

Except I'm listening anyway & making
meaning where I want to find it.
Probably your message is hardscrabble
libertarian individualism: *Make do now.*
Make do now. Those not born to a fine nest
can live under a rock, there's always something.

Well, to hell with you, bird.
Here's what I'm hearing:
Keep pecking, keep turning shit over.
Don't stop singing because the vultures
circle overhead—they love sucking blood,
they will eat their own before it's over.
Be ready. Be ready. Be ready.

The Donkey on the Road

Each year I cut a tree sprout from the chimney
of my old house, and always it grew again,
a little broader and leafier each time.

Nothing prepares me for anything else, though
this sound of water gasping and sputtering
in the coffee maker doesn't surprise me,

or the springs in my daughter's bed releasing
as she gets up to brush her teeth before school,
feeling her way through the new house, the fresh life.

Our dog's untrimmed nails click across the hardwoods
and as I open the door, the paradise
some are promised flashes brightly through the grass.

The donkey on the road to Brementown meets
his crew of cast-outs, no sorrier than most,
none really the musicians they pretend to be.

I left the tree in the chimney and came here,
my new destination as good as Bremen,
as worthy as the home I have set out from.

Emissaries

Some mornings when I'm reading
early, no light yet but the table lamp,
my left hand will run through scales
along the spine of the open book.
My hands keep their own remembrance
buried in fine grooves of flesh.
The fingers turn over ignitions, faucets,
always attuned to their proper force,
knuckles never breaking things
unless my brain overpowers them.
They've discovered spectacular terrains,
soft enclosures I can never enter again.
I send them ahead as scouts for survey,
emissaries that flip the lights
in every dark hallway of the future.

Bayou Storm

One entire summer in New Orleans, mornings broke open
like fresh eggs, cracked and spilled into a blue bowl of sky.

I drank coffee over the kitchen sink, watching sunlight glisten
across roof shingles as far north as the Fairgrounds.

Some days I smelled the horses making their early sprints.
Third-floor apartment of the tallest house on Crete Street—

I could see the pressbox and the empty top row of bleachers.

By noon the heat was a second suit of clothes, and by mid-day
the first drops of rain sizzled on the sidewalks.

A storm would erupt, then subside just as quickly, the dead crustacean
smell swirling, and finally the air cool enough to breathe again.

Then one day I awoke to rattling glass, and the quiet morning
had crossed over. Clouds rolled in the color of concrete.

The electricity blinked out with the first wave of thunder
and I watched as lightning skipped across the city.

Water stood and rippled in the street for an hour
then streamed off underground.

Nothing moved on Esplanade as I crossed toward Bayou St. John—
Saturday, 10:00 AM and already the air ruptured.

I could smell espresso and fresh bread at CC's Coffee House,
where I stopped and caught my breath, but didn't go in,
walking instead up DeSoto, past the mute houses.

A man opened a fence and carried some branches to the curb.
He shrugged and smiled.

The Bayou never gleamed beautifully as it curled through Mid-City,
but this morning the bowels of every Mississippi River tributary
south of Minnesota seemed flushed into New Orleans.

Hurricane Katrina was two years away, but I could see the future
in miniature spinning upstream in the murk—

Dry socket of a war just begun, blood and oil swirling together,
everyone feeling wire-tapped, no child left behind, and across town
the lower Ninth Ward strapped to the mast of a ship not yet sinking—

A mud-slaked turtle swiveled past in the current, dragged into the light,
as though the whole floor of the river had been swept up,
                              with no place to settle but the back of my throat.

Elemental Study

I

All the windows open, a radio on the floor
scattering quick notes from *Charlie Parker*
at Storyville, the room off-balance,
smoke, paint, August heat, turpentine.
Jason circled the easel for perspective,
like the strategic dance of a featherweight
searching for the perfect uppercut angle.
He loved the brush as he hated his father—
purely and without sublimation:
violence without cruelty,
breaking the neck off a bottle once
when we had lost the opener.

II

That year at Labor Day we watched a blaring
smoke-tinted fireworks display launched
into the night sky from Henley Street Bridge.
We waded through drunks and security cops
down to the edge of the blackened river,
our bloodstreams muddled and toxic.
The air hissed and melted into glowering fog,
fallen cinder drifting like a tarp on the water.
For the duration of roaring marches and explosions
we formed a still-life: image for the coarse-grained
canvas he later smeared with a ground mixture—
coriander, cigarette tobacco, garden mulch,
stolen iris flowers, titled *Rough Composition*.

Wrightsville Beach

Up early for a walk by the fishing boats,
tracing your initials and mine in the foam
of low tide, its spool of dark thread
arriving like the wet shadows of clouds.
Three red echoes of light in the harbor,
only sign of life beyond the smashed pier,
entrance roped off, furthest quarter lost,
splintered legposts jutting from the waves.
Shells the size of baseballs pock-marked
the sand, their uneven curves preserved,
concentric ridges crusted with salt-grit.
One found the soft skin above my heel,
pink-lobed conch shell—
            crescent moon imprint, blood tattoo.
I brought that shell home, and now it sits
harmless on my desk beside a picture of you.
I wonder if I could find your name written
between hymns to Rilke and the Red Sox
in my misplaced journal of those seaside days,
when I sensed you a rising presence,
tropical depression bearing in off the coast.

Time and the Motions Our Bodies Made

Waves of rock and roll moved through us,
guitars barely kept in tune, singers slurring
laments and praises to improvident affections.

We danced whether we believed in the lyrics
or not, because the rhythm turned us into ancient
ciphers, in control of time but surrendered in body

to ritual movement, it protected us from the specter
of parents, how our lives could evolve into theirs.
The years together since then have drained away

more quickly than the cold bottles we shifted from
hand to hand, so unprepared for the requirements
that money would make on us, the doing without,

gleaning through the lean life of words and pictures.
We stepped out of the Mercury or Barley & Hops
smelling like cigarette ash and breathing in as much

clean air as our lungs would hold, our ears ringing
like the night itself was an amplifier, and we were
the music it blasted out across invisible currents.

The Road into the Lake

Here among sandstone ledges and mussel shells
a wide set of cement steps ascends to nothing,
leads to the front door to a drowned house,
the ghost of a road tracing into the shallow
middle of Norris Lake, toward an island rising

like the iron arches of a fallen bridge.
Strange things surface in a drought:
the block foundation of Doc Palmer's house
where it sank in 1936, before he delivered
my mother and my father into their lives.

I cannot picture the walls as they stood then
any more than I can see the lumberyard
on the bank of Clinch River, where my
great-grandfather strung timber into log rafts,
somewhere now under the lake's gravity.

This world before my world, beyond recovery,
how many times have I stared into the surface
and wondered where they worked, played marbles
and baseball, and stabled their horses? And why?
Why keep asking these questions of the water

which can reveal nothing of those days?
There may be some fiber or platelet circulating
through me that knows why my people came here,
why they stayed—the last ones to leave
were born too late to know the first to arrive,

that's how long the line stretched unbroken,
seven generations by the river in Capps' Creek,
but when the last to leave finally left,
they scattered like dandelion pistils
to Michigan, California, all over.

Yet some stayed as near as the government
would allow them, just across pine ridges
and creeks to form their own Tennessee valley
authority, where my father later brought me
to catch bluegill and small-mouthed bass,

or tie on a lead sinker and cast deep for catfish.
My line never went far enough, but it was
the casting that mattered, the being small there
with my father and my uncles, standing as near
as we could to land we would never inherit.

I searched the red silt for horse shoes or shards
of their coffee cups, then as now looking for the past
to appear like stacked ledges of clouds
mirroring off water, the imprint of our ancestors
stamped into the grain of my sifting hands.

Morning Sky, September 2001

A clamor of bells from the clocktower,
                        Sunday in late morning.
The chapel organ sends up a prelude—
I think it's Bach, mournful for early autumn,
Sixteenth of September,
My step a sidewalk shadow lost in a bellchime.

A hundred years ago Dutch elms lined this walk.
In photographs they tower above all of Ithaca,
Domed crowns of libraries and stone lecture halls,
                        Morning sky powders through the leaves.

A marker planted on East Avenue reads *Hofstader Elms.*
No one alive on this earth today stood in their broad shadows.
Hold the pictures to light and they lose an edge,
The fine serrations on the downturned leaves
                        Blur into late last night, early this morning.
Standing there as the blight eats into their roots.

Buildings collapse and three thousand souls are lifted,
Each alone, into God's vast marrow.

Sleep hardly resembles itself with that constant image,
                        Late last night turning over
And around, becoming this moment here on the sidewalk,
Morning started, Sage Chapel filling with soft voices.

Buildings collapse and the world's great inventions collide,
Planes and towers, speed and architecture,
The message that says the center cannot hold:
                        Twilight times.
What's so frightening about twilight? Indistinct lines.

Five days later and the rubble smolders and groans,
                        The sky still erupts into furious welcome.

Understory

Cold morning, upstate premiere of May, two dogs
chasing down the slope toward the water.

Sky and lake, mist over mistfall's shadow,
all color lapsed into countless gray strands,

one shade dark as a finely cased bullet,
the next faded as slide locks on windows

of the chained-up Ithaca Gun Factory.
I've stood beside Cayuga Lake on the rocks

watching wind steer circles on the surface,
crest and wave, the opposite bank a thumb-print.

Two young dogs at play in a field, not here,
but in the meadow behind my great-uncle Joe's

fallen barn, a morning twenty years past,
lodged between the eye and memory's socket.

*   *   *

A golden age, a blue-eyed shepherd and a mutt
running beside a boy, seen by no one then,

by no one now, except a grown man looking
across a lake eight hundred miles from that field.

A rabbit bolts from the fencerow and the dogs
take off. There he stands, his hands on a rail

split by some great-great-grandfather long ago,
a name nearly lost and a face he cannot picture,

never photographed, never made part of the record.

A glacial shift gouged them out of flat lands,
eleven long scars filled as deep as Lake Ontario,

gifts of the ice age, splintered bones, Finger Lakes,
fished by the Iroquois who tended their banks.

This year's ice age held until early spring,
yet leaves struggle forth on the oaks and maples

to tremble in the wind, a cold surge I can feel
through sub-layers of my skin, follicles of my hair.

Nothing aches like home, and how the slow hours
traveled to get here from there turn into years,

the full weight of stone between my native foothills,
understory of the oldest mountains on earth,

and the northern broadening out of Appalachia,
time flattening toward the absence of it all.

Not here. Not on the rocky bank of Cayuga Lake,
shaken loose by a steady throb of the jet stream.

Not by the ruins of an ancient barn, one dog rolled
under a car, the other shot by a prick on a motorbike.

Not even in the library, between thumb-weathered
board-backings that hold secrets written to water,

diary of a week on the Concord and Merrimack rivers,
elegy for a lost brother, a vision of time suspended,

words that do not answer the question I cannot form:
some mix of whereness and now, thisness and then,

never wherever I am, and not part of the record.

III

For Richard Wilbur

I

Most days stray off in the tread and retread
of history, in calendars passing through
their cycles, spent in the practical use

we make of them. Books and trivia shows
keep some dates alive to recall an event,
but for March 1, 1921, I find only the birth

of Richard Wilbur to mark its passage.
In the back corner of the house where I grew up,
called the brown room for its chestnut walls,

Edith Reva Johnson was born the same day,
my mother's mother, into a place hardly noted
on any map, hardly reached by any road.

II

When I was a boy, she would walk with me
over the cattle trail through old woods
between our large house and her small one—

she called it Indian's Warpath for the arrowheads
we found, and in the undergrowth she picked leaves
that made the best medicines, heart-leaf, rat's vein,

the billow of lamb's ear, spidery streaked leaf,
wild ginger to flavor the whiskey, rock candy,
and glycerin cough syrup I dreaded in winter.

Her kindnesses were small and made no fuss—
quarters wrapped in tin foil slipped into my hand
when I was home from college—birth gave her

no comforts but a large family to be hungry with.
Most days she kept to herself, and the boy
at the window was me, hoping she would appear.

III

Their lives begun together in baleful Ides,
Wilbur's spent rendering the arc of lines
etched in the faces of baroque wall fountains,

immersed in the transformations of art.
Angels appeared to him in the laundry,
calling him to come out and love the world.

My grandmother rode the scab bus to her
first job, where she glazed porcelain conductors
to crown the tops of telephone poles, then

she stooped for years to empty garbage cans
in hospital waiting rooms, her steely gray
hair cut short and bound in a blue plastic cap.

IV

Wilbur dug his rows in the old field of verse,
tending a corner of ground some thought
fallow, used up, but look now at the clean

scaffolding of his crops, vibrant and green.
His poems have flourished beyond their plot;
they trade for coins to stock the Muse's purse.

V

As the mind reader tells us, some things are truly lost,
details of an entire life plunging down the haggard
escarpments of misfiring neurotransmitters.

When my grandmother's mind began to vacate,
it left a little at a time, closing random doors
in the storehouse of memories she maintained for us,

dropping what she knew about cures in the foliage,
about how her mother thinned their beans with water,
added the breakfast grease so nothing went to waste.

She is truly lost, the woman who named me, her breath,
her body, the stories she rarely told about herself,
the unknown, never-praised, backward girl of springtime.

The Pier at 5 AM

Archilochus, political fragment 105

The first glimmer of it, purpling of the black—
That's why I woke you—
Morning a present we might open together.

*Glaucus, see, the waves are rising and the deep
        sea is disturbed;*

Lisa, lost in the deep rushing of dreams,
I have come down to you, bringing nothing

Except the promise of a spreading light
                            beyond the pier.

Sea and sky fold into one dark hanging.

                    *   *   *

*All about the heights of Gyrae stands a towering
        mass of cloud—
            I fall a prey to unexpected fear.*

Rain slants through us and we walk into its wet arms,
Into the quiet of our separate selves,
The mists of indifference, a lowering mass of cloud.

Can the second life of love begin this way?

Pass beyond stinging eyes and wringing shirts?
Read these lines against the years, the unexpected fear—
I woke you to call you back,
                            we let go too soon,
High tide surges in, but we have all this—
A day identical to night, wet darkness to begin again.

Wild Strawberries at St. Mary's Hospital

After a long stagger through gleaming tiles and interlocking hallways,
Through a glassed in walkway between buildings,
Fighting off a milky, breaded, cafeteria smell,

I followed your singing to a concrete bench beside a flower garden:

A pair of bright red heads peering out of the mulch,
Two wild strawberries grown in the sculpted domestic beds,
Ignoring me from beneath the shrubbery's damp morning webs.

Why so quiet now? Mute messengers, you've lost your nerve.

You live in the shadows of plastic-looking purple and yellow tulips.
An affront to hospital groundskeepers, the surgeons of the soil.

Summer air idling around us in the roar of central cooling units.

You were one of the disappointments of my childhood.

Scattered beautifully at the corners of the yard where I built castles,
In fields where we spread salt for the lumbering cows,
Along the road banks covered with gravel dust.

I defied my mother who said, they're pretty but you can't eat them.

You twisted my mouth into a ribbon, made my eyes stream,
Left a bitter burning film on my tongue all day.

I don't believe you called me here to tell me anything good.
.
You're not supposed to be here—you're an irregularity,
A blemish, a spot on the x-ray of the hospital's controlled space.

When I try to picture you as a sign of hope, of happy remembrance,
I recall a scene from a subtitled black and white movie:

An old man visits his childhood home and remembers his love
For a young cousin, a Swedish maiden in a summer dress,
How they picked wild strawberries together by a lake.

The pair coming back inside to a fine meal, a happy clucking family.

And then I remember his dream of the clock with no hands,
The death carriage in an empty street, his own body revealed.

Late morning scrolling past and I can't go back inside.
My uncle is in there, beginning the dying that I knew
Would happen, that I knew I would run away from.

Life unfolding on a screen, real time and false space. Ever unfolding.

Piano Key

Corner fixture in the attic, collector of light debris,
Bookshelf for old home décor magazines,
My grandmother's unpolished piano.
Banged on by three generations of children,
None learning the notes, the scales, its life within.

No one mentions her playing, though the keys
Lost their gloss somehow.
                    My father's mother.
She mostly seemed small and quiet, always old,
Old her whole life, only speaking to say what hurts.
Abandoned after her ninth child was born,
Sent home to her own mother.

I plunk my way left to right, up from the deep-forest
Bass notes toward the bright high registers,
Just past middle C, a dead spot I remember as a child,
                    A crucial note that will not sing.

Little key, did she bring you to life with a touch,
Same as she did my father?
                    Were you part of a night time song
She kneaded into dreams for her sleeping children?
Song I'll never hear, white peg bent to silence.

Reservation Snapshot

The rest of the day must have held a long drive
out of the mountains, dreams of battles waged
with arrows from the saddles of white horses.
I knew where all the American Indian tribes
lived, how they painted their bodies for war,
the number of miles on the Trail of Tears.
The crooked roads and steep inclines carried us
back down to the life we have each lived since,
the wandering and drift, slow years opening out
past childhood's end and youth's front range.

A Cherokee in buckskin stands beside me,
flashes a serious face for my mother's camera.
Carolina mountain peaks rise up behind us
and dissolve in a blue drapery of fog,
but the boy I was then looks out as though
he could see for miles, like he's just spotted
signal fires from the nearest village.
Seven years old, sitting on a towering white horse,
his shirt clings to him in the drizzling rain,
the bright feathers of his head-dress glisten.

Devil's Snuff

My cousin David and I made sport of it,
Ranging into the woods to see who
Could turn up the most,
                    then smashed our shoes
Down on the knobby brown heads of dust—

The devil felt so real to me that I trembled a little
At the spores spreading wide in the air,
His hot breath breaking
                    loose upon the earth,
Our laughter another sign that he owned us.

Facing West from Cumberland Gap

—after Robert Morgan

Having followed the circling road
Up through damp fronds of early fog,
You might stand beside the chain-rock
And look over steep ridge faces,
Across miles and years receding

To D. Boone's vision of the West:
Black bears roaming the underbrush,
Ribbons of trout threading clear streams,
Old growth stands of white oak, poplar.
The chestnuts and wild peavines now

Vanished from these hills, from the wells
Of their oldest soul's memory.
The land existed outside all
Money and accounts, no ledger
Except time's steady deduction.

The Motherland of the forest
Calls some of us still; we answer
With the best sounds we can summon,
Echo back the birdsong's bequest,
To let each be what each will be.

Trade

Land swells and sinkholes forced hard angles
in the roads, some just swatches through thicket
and brush patch, others graded with gravel—
those leading to zinc mines or river dock.
After dark, the ringing pitch of an engine,
slack and surge, slapshifted through the gears
toward blacktop, clear liquor in the trunk
sloshing against the tin lids of mason jars.

Horn Rogers in a black-primered Mercury,
stub-nosed pistol riding on the bench seat.
He'd pull around back of the brewery
where bank fires were always lit, and meet
Elzo Miller, who paid cash at the asking price,
who knew quality was its own device.

The driest cavewalls beneath Weaver's Knob
lined three deep with charred white oak barrels.
Still hutches buried in the deepest pinewoods,
where noon gets no lighter that the last hour
of midnight's keeping. Artesian wellspring
piped from an abandoned marble quarry,
water streaming cold through copper lining—
corn distillate with no sweetness lost to vapor.

Revivals

The finest days of summer passed along
with no effort at all—they opened up warm,
got brighter through the hours, and closed down
to the various singings and scrapings of night.
Any resistance came from us, the whole family
wishing and denying, turning on each other.

My job was to talk with the doctors, research
the incurable, find whatever comfort reason offered.
It was the worst job. I envied his sisters,
my fawning aunts, who drove him to revivals,
brought him under the hands of those who said,
"Drink and ye shall be healed."

So he drank and prayed and made great donations
and erratic cells still shot out into every organ
until we had nothing left but a morphine pump,
a damp cloth, and windows open all night.
No faith, no reason, my uncle grappling
after his breath, and me trying to hold it for him.

Little Girl and the Dreadful Snake

Cotton rolled his own cigarettes
and made other simple things—
a pantry cabinet for his sister's preserves,
and a Hawaiian-style slide guitar
that he strummed with a milk jug lid
as he sang us cautionary ballads.

He was my mother's favorite uncle,
so no one talked about his woodstove
churning through the middle of summer,
his religious conversations with the television,
or that he hadn't ridden in a car in eleven years.

My cousins and I gathered in a half-moon
around him, and shivered at the warnings
he sang to us against playing in deep woods
where dreadful snakes liked to sleep,
because terrible things happened to children,
especially when they thought they were safe.

Each of his bedrooms was wallpapered
with jigsaw puzzles, thousand piece
replicas of the Eiffel Tower,
a panorama of the Great Wall of China
beside young thoroughbreds in racing gear.

Once my pulse surged to see my own face,
with my mother and sister in an unframed
Polaroid, taped to the wall among the rest
of Cotton's widely extended family, the Mount
Rushmore faces of our great Americans
and the folded glowing hands of Jesus Christ.

Water Washing Away

Early summer, late afternoon,
sky stretching into its long recline,
  the lighter blue blanching to white.

Our garden hose sprouts puddles
in the yard, and Chloe splashes through
  them. She's ten years old,

but for the moment I see her at half
that age, running under a sprinkler
  in a seahorse swimsuit

the first summer we moved into the house,
her fear of water washing away,
  such small feet tamping the ground.

I should make her shut off the faucet,
wasting water in a dry month,
  driving up a dreadful utility bill,

but I'll pay it off, I think to the wind,
with these silver coins the late sun
  scatters in drops across the grass,

A fair price for the vision of a girl
who has warped the ancient spell of time,
  who has turned back my eyes,

almost to her birth again, then into my own
fading childhood, rewinding years that even
  the sun's bright currency cannot purchase.

Mother's Milk

A couple of things she gave me:
powdered formula mixed with water
heated on a stove but held very near
her heart, she said, while I drank it;
the certainty that Jimmy Carter
should have been president for life
and that a yellow dog would be better
for poor people than Ronald Reagan.

                    *   *   *

By the time I was born, we had moved
back to Sharps Chapel and taken over
my great-grandfather's old house.
My mother directed the small ensemble
of our family: her kind sister, alone
with three kids in a falling-down house;
her uncle, speaking mostly to relatives
already dead; an aunt across the ridge
whose husband tried to shoot my brother.
My older brother and sister, crashing and
dreaming their way through high school.
My father parked his rig one day a week
to clear fields or fix the ancient tractor.
And me, the youngest by eleven years,
born in the vacuum of her father's early death.

                    *   *   *

I stepped out of the airport in Syracuse
into the first darts of a swirling snow
the whole western skyline dropping fast
back in lake effect country
$38 in my wallet
alone and wishing for home

Sunday after Thanksgiving

*   *   *

Once I tripped over a barbed wire fence,
both legs tangled between the strands,
six years old, struck down by the first
mountain I thought I could climb.
She carried me home, my shins wrapped
in a t-shirt and my ear close against her pulse,
tears starting to dry on both our faces.

*   *   *

A few other things she gave me:

an ear for slightly off-pitch singing
notes left lingering in throats
from Loretta Lynn to Lucinda Williams—

unwavering loyalty to women who wear
choppy haircuts and just-visible tattoos
and who pay half-interested attention to me—

an avalanche of love and kindness
the best preparation a man
can get for this world's embrace.

The Upper Ridge

> How it is Night–in Nest and Kennel–
> And where was the Wood–
> Just a dome of Abyss is Bowing
> Into Solitude–
> —Emily Dickinson

We had worked the daylight down to its ember,
dragging dropped limbs out the fencerow
and mending each frozen strand we could stretch

back to a post. My father twisted the wire
barehanded: tiny curls of skin gathered
around the barbs into papery wings,

stemless florets, ray flower, kin of the dogwood.

What startles about December snow is how it quiets.
Ice is opposite, each step we took
cracked sharp as our mallet ringing the spikes

as they reached deep into the split cedar posts.

As we topped the upper ridge, "Lord, God"
was all my father said. Down the slope
I could see the red and white bull calf,

his body splayed over the frozen pond,
forelegs thrown out like a yield sign.
We each held silent and still, the sky lowered,

taste of rusted nailheads sour on my teeth.

A sound like the rustle of barn swallows
echoed through the measure of my solitude,
my father gone for a rope and peg,

I was on my knees beside the crusted water,
searching the frosted eyes for a glimpse
into another world, my cheek drawn down

by the pull of moisture and something else,
something closing the inches between
my face and the sound of bells ringing

from the dark crust nearest the pond floor.

IV

Field Portrait

The man and woman stand knee-deep in grass,
each balancing a small girl like a school prize.
The man is tall and leans toward the camera
while the child in his arms looks down,
squinting at the tiny flares of her sunlit shoes.
A wooden fence stretches out behind them
in a row of short sticks, like tobacco spears
snapped in half, around a small orchard
of heavy-bearing apple trees and pear trees.

The woman's dress is the same color as the pears
and it must be Sunday, for the fabric is neither
muslin nor floursack, but looks to be fine as linen
with a flower embroidery stitched along the hemline.
She does not lean in to close the circle
                              and she does not smile,
though the children beam like lit candles,
their dresses white as cinder fallen from the sun.

A drunkard's like a chimney full of ashes,
more likely to burn the house down
than keep it warm. That's what her mother said
when she confessed they were getting married.
She had thought it over and over, a man can change—
she had seen him in the field; he could outwork
his mule when it came to plowing corn rows,
could sow six acres of rye grass in a day.

The pencil trace says, Edith and Ken, Summer 1943.

It is not hard to imagine how the man's body
would turn on itself in the years to follow,
become a natural enemy of his ways and wants.
Spinal declension, eruptions of the stomach,
                              sotted liver, stroke.
He never got the farm he worked those years,
got none of the money his father made
when he sold it, none of the tools or cattle.

In the picture, one happy daughter reaches up
to the apples hanging like Christmas bulbs

while the other, my mother, looks at the ground.
Their young father, teller of heroic Indian tales,
drinker of cough syrup and rubbing alcohol,
stands with them, his life more than half over.
Their mother never relenting, who will later stab
his lip with a fork, beat him sober with a boot-heel,
call him the saintliest no-account man
                     God ever set upon the earth.

Late Summer Woodcut

We waited until nearly sunset before
picking up our knives and heading out.
I watched my uncle's fingers
through the late brink of light
working over the rough cedar stick
with a black-handled Barlow,
the blade no wider than his thumb.
Purple shavings curled away toward
the grass and into the folds of his jacket.
Their scent reminded me of a toychest
filled with metal airplanes, each one
marked with an allied flag on its wing.

He showed me the test of a knife,
razing hair along the back of his hand.
Each of us knew the practical truth,
what happens when it gets in your lungs,
how the menace multiplies and eats through.
We needed a long talk about the disease,
chemistry and radiation, what to hope against,
before the cool September night drove us inside.
Starlings flocked to the trees behind us,
their wings beating heavily as a thunderstorm,
I took their whistles and clicks for song,
listening for a message, some secret release.

Our breath fogged the air and to see it
come to life, a presence right before us,
amplified the settling darkness—
this is all there is, all we are: without it, nothing.
A smooth circle suddenly took shape
at the stick's slender end and each flick
of his knife revealed a deeper stroke of color,
the heart of the wood emerging.

My Sister at Sea

Autumn shakes the air above Cayuga Lake,
Snapping willow fronds like lofted green flags.
Reading your recent letter threatens to break
My grip, spreading memory's loose bags
Before me, us at the ocean, my first glimpse
Of boundless water, barely five years old,
You swimming out, then under, a full eclipse
That made my gut sink, fingers turn cold.
The thought of losing you shot through me then
Just as it does now, wishing I could bring
You here to this shore, that we might amend
Some old ritual, a spell of un-doing:
Make your illness a small boat we could burn,
Sailing out in ashes on the current.

Temper in a Time of War

In and out of conversation all day, mind drifting against the present,
Into my fist slamming against the dining room table this morning,
Enraged at your willfulness, your spite, lack of order.
Instead of repeating the whole fight, I see just one scene,
Envisioning only the moment when you withered
In shock at my voice spinning sideways toward you.

To be eight years old through the twilight of a great country,
Torn out of your trust by one you are supposed to trust~
Towering over you, that's how I felt at the table.
Together but scattered into as many particles as the humming air.

I notice how you listen to the world, asking me what
Insurgents means. Your ear tuned to a tragedy we didn't create,
Intuition telling you it's worse than I would have you believe.
In and out of conversation, my mind drifting always back to you.

Vista

Any day like this one, standing beside water,
Sunset glancing through the wind,
Like Cezanne painted it, like he tried to say,
Pink ripples through me but it cannot talk.

The clear vista of years seems to scatter—
I cannot hold the pleasures in mind
From evenings at home on the old Sundays.
Morning slips past, words block

Their own saying, words that matter
Rise up to speak and are denied.
Born once to the world, once taken away,
My mother, dear ship, sail, sea, dock.

Search Program

Something else must have woken me,
But nothing stirred in the dark room,
So the mockingbirds' frenzied music
Fixed my attention. I understood nothing
But the urgency of the message.
The door back into my dream closed
And I could not even remember what
I wanted to rush back to, the blank excitement
Extending the muscles in my fingers.
Lying in a floating body, my eyes blinking,
The circuitry of my nerves clicking, combustion
Of blood through tubes and tissue.
Folded deep into the nest of it all,
Birds call out from electrical wires
Crisscrossed above the flowering dogwoods,
Codes unspooling without human sympathy.

Equations

In the afternoon light a red bird
drops to a low poplar limb
and eyes the mounted feeder,
depleted since morning,
then just hangs steady,
pivoting his tufted head.
Late winter and he is brighter
than my daughter's wagon
parked beside the plank fence.
He becomes still, his black face
aimed directly at my window.
He rustles but doesn't fly.
I know I am looking into something
I have seen before, a memory
rising from the substrata,
when he bolts for higher branches
and joins a half dozen other cardinals.
I lose him in the crowd
of lapsed recognitions,
where he glides among the names
of English sea captains
and the sizes of Detroit engine blocks,
floating past batting averages from
the 1982 Atlanta Braves,
and equations for measuring
the velocity of falling bodies.

The Wilderness Trail

—For Chloe

1.

Winter arrived in the night
and hung heavy in yellow pines.
No one knew it was coming,
so I woke up with expectations
of canned pineapples and toast,
a dark trudge to catch the schoolbus.

2.

The morning had fallen white
and I went out to find animal prints,
a feathered tomahawk humming
in the belt loop of my blue jeans.
I had left the expedition and the outpost
to find what only Boone would recognize.

3.

I walked past the barn and my father's
David Brown tractor under the loft,
into the woods and back through time.
Wind twisted and I curled inside my jacket—
I looked around and saw nothing human,
nothing made, two long centuries elapsed.

4.

Sparrows and jays skittered under the cedars,
and I followed a trail through the soft
underbrush, setting out for the far horizon,
two biscuits with bacon tucked in my pocket.
The long shadow of Cumberland Mountain
hiding the deep trace of Cumberland Gap.

Nightjar Songs

A truck hammers off in the distance, accelerates
East toward Asheville, Smoky Mountain foothills.
The night moves out with it, but not so steadily:
Asleep by seven-thirty, awake at eleven,
Still awake at one-thirty, at two. Does the moon
Keep me up, loud, bright, insistently full?
Wondering how to pay the electric bill?
My daughter at six still refusing to read,
Pleading that she was born with an animal spirit?
The engine rattle fades and I step down to the grass.
Two nightjar songs: one a low constant tone,
The other a rising note, then silence, then rising.
October's music.
Oak leaves, early fallen, sparkling across the yard,
All of it a feast, almost a pattern, almost design.

Wellsprings

We turned the lake's slow surface to bright spanners
With our underwater lures and orange-cap floaters.

Big Ellum, Lead Mine Bend, Capps' Creek,
Artesian Wellsprings, behind the old house seat,

Flatwoods, Lost Creek, Palmer's Junction,
Forks of the River, Mining Dump, Bridgetown.

We cast for bluegill, mostly, and hoped for bass,
Since half as many would make twice the catch—

Our goal was supper, but we rarely earned that keep,
My uncle and I. Though we slung our lines to the deep

Middle of Norris Lake, a hot afternoon on the shady
Banks of a hidden cove was reward enough, our muddy

Shoes left in the bed of the truck while we waded the shore
Looking for arrowheads or fossil rocks. When we got bored,

We propped the reels on forked sticks so Gerald could smoke
And play *Waylon and Willie* as I sipped a warm bottle of Coke,

Rummaged the glove-box for places he'd been, matchbooks
From the Amarillo Armadillo, Flying J Truckstop, and Rook's.

Those nights we fished until dark were better than a child's
Christmas in Wales, to be eight, mid-summer, home in the wild.

Echolalia

White ash cradled in the fire grate
        still warm, a hollow body,

              seething ancient whispers,

lost language.

Chloe speaks, then the words speak again,
        second sounds barely catching waves—

              untold meanings float between us,

pockets of air tremble with the unknown.

Speaks then listens. Echolalia, her caged words.

Does the mind suspect betrayal in the throat?

              *   *   *

Walk past it in the woods and you might mistake
the white ash for a hickory, with the same leaf-bunches,
same bone-colored bark, but don't be fooled—
you can know the ash by the length of its scars.
It looks burned already.

              *   *   *

Chloe climbs and never looks down. She finds a perch
between branches, feathered in a bright red waistcoat.
Her eyes skip the middle distance, scan the horizon.
She's seven years old, thirty feet in the air.

                    *   *   *

I speak to the animals, she says, they know my heart.

                    *   *   *

The meaning in our lives usually stands right beside us.
We might pick it up and carry it into the light,

            lift it to a higher seat, but we never own it.

What another person's life meant at one moment,

            a speck on the continuum,

gave us our birth, and the body we pull away from it.

We answer to the name, yet never know the trail it moves along.

                    *   *   *

When leaves whisper in the wind, she quiets,
            her lips move but make no sound,

some private language threads out through her limbs.

What Chloe hears hangs before me, a stretched canvas
        she works at with delicate gestures,
                    her brush never touching the surface.

Deep Corner

Impossible to defend,
drop step and ball fake,
shoulders squared
then fade away.
Fingertip release.
My brother's move,
best thing
he ever taught me.

I dribbled the grass
out of the ground
every day after school,
bare patch in the side yard
becoming a great coliseum.

My two shots:
fade-away jumper
and three-pointer
from the deep corner.
I'd bounce myself a pass,
catch and shoot
in one motion,
nine in a row, ten in a row,
easy as free throws.

My brother grown,
sewing shirts all day
at Standard Knitting Mill,
having his own kids,
while I worked on the moves,
shooting into the night,

Everything dark
except the white nylon threads
swinging beneath the rim,
and the moon-spiked caps of clover
shining up through the grass.
The ball spinning an arc
against gravity,
as my fingertips buzz,
the net shushing back to me.

Big Elm Point

I sat on the bank until everyone else stopped caring
whether we caught any fish, until it was clear
they weren't biting, wouldn't take a red worm
if it swam right into their suction-cup mouths.
My daughter had gone off to line up her horses
over the sandstone outcroppings that made
such perfect mountains for the animals
to struggle across.
                  I wanted in on that game,
to be face to face with Chloe's serious eyes,
portraying the bravest stallion who leads
his herd to safety from lurking wranglers
and mountain lions. I wanted to follow
my mother and father through the field
toward the old Stiner Cemetery lot,
study the gravestones over the nineteenth century
bones that tended the land before its two rivers
were neutered into this slow cresting lake.

I wanted to go examine the weathering trunk
of the fallen elm that gave this point
its enduring name, Big Elm, pronounced *Ellum*
by everyone I ever heard say it.
I wanted to think about why no drunken fishermen
had chopped it into firewood and grilled
their catch over the ghosts of its resin.
            To imagine the living tree, and to remember
the mornings in third grade when I cried because
I dreaded Mrs. Sharp and her gingham dresses,
how I prayed when the school bus brought us
into view that her blue Ford LTD wouldn't be parked
at the end of Sharps Chapel Elementary.
How one morning my mother took pity on me,
drove us past the school to Brantley's Market
where we got a bag of peanuts and two Cokes,
and took us to Big Ellum Point where she
let me throw rocks into the water until noon.

At nine years old nothing made me happier
than my father bringing home a new lure
from White's Truck Stop at Raphine, Virginia,
or for my Uncle Gerald to get home from work
and say, *Let's go cast a line before it gets too dark.*

Late spring evenings arrived like birds landing,
and the full span of summer reached out
for us, waving like the cattails I tried to catch
from the car window as the gravel rolled us past.
The hours creeping, sunset alive over the trees,
while the years folded up as quickly as notebook
paper drawn thick with pictures of muscle cars
and basketball logos, pages folded up and gone,
tucked into the pockets of our blue jeans.

I wanted to swim back from those cast-away days,
the wash of the past, and on with the present,
but I couldn't take my eyes off the fishing line.
The water hardly moved unless I reeled in
and split the surface with my floater,
looking perfectly still though moving without cease,
                    does that sound like water or time?
I threw out, reeled in, and watched the orange eye
staring back at me for three solid hours
before it finally bounced and raced under.
All the other things I could be doing, and I watched
the empty hook glisten back through the water.
A pair of Canada geese came jeering over us
and splashed down in the opposite cove—
the ferry operator packed up his thermos
as the elms and poplars spread out their
long shadows across the rim of Norris Lake.

So much was happening, the evening so alive
in its subtle approach, that I hardly noticed
the second bob of the floater, the fresh and writhing
worm casting its ancient spell, but the fish bit hard
and raced so that I could hardly lose it this time.
                    All I had to do was hold on
until Chloe came with her net and brought him up
into the air, a bluegill twice the size of her palm.

How beautifully the hook slid out of his lip,
how clean he looked in her tentative hands
glittering in the late sun, the hour of Cezanne,
hour of golden spilling,
                    the silken arc as she tossed him
back toward the rest of his silvery-blue life.